The SMART Interview Playbook

Mastering Winning Strategies for 2025 and Beyond

CONSULTORIA IA

Table of Contents

Brief Overview

Why Read this Book

Target Audience

Prologue: The Interview Revolution

Chapter 1: Unlocking the SMART Interview Secret: Proven Strategies That Work

Chapter 2: The Art of Answering with Impact: Winning Over Interviewers with Memorable Responses

Chapter 3: Beyond the Résumé: Building Your Personal Brand to Stand Out in 2025 and Beyond

Chapter 4: "The SMART Method in Action: Essential Q&A Strategies to Shine"

Chapter 5: Playing to Win: Mastering Virtual Interviews and AI-Powered Assessments

Appendices

The SMART Interview Playbook

Mastering Winning Strategies for 2025 and Beyond

CONSULTORIA IA

CONSULTORIA IA

The SMART Interview Playbook

Mastering Winning Strategies for 2025 and Beyond

Copyright © 2024 by Consultoria IA

All rights reserved. No part of this publication may be reproduced, stored or transmitted in any form or by any means, electronic, mechanical, photocopying, recording, scanning, or otherwise without written permission from the publisher. It is illegal to copy this book, post it to a website, or distribute it by any other means without permission.

First edition

This book was professionally typeset on Reedsy
Find out more at reedsy.com

Contents

Brief Overview

Why Read this Book

Target Audience

Prologue: The Interview Revolution

Chapter 1: Unlocking the SMART Interview Secret: Proven Strategies That Work

Chapter 2: The Art of Answering with Impact: Winning Over Interviewers with Memorable Responses

Chapter 3: Beyond the Résumé: Building Your Personal Brand to Stand Out in 2025 and Beyond

Chapter 4: "The SMART Method in Action: Essential Q&A Strategies to Shine"

Chapter 5: Playing to Win: Mastering Virtual Interviews and AI-Powered Assessments

Appendices

Brief Overview

The SMART Interview Playbook: Mastering Winning Strategies for 2025 and Beyond

In today's fast-paced, ever-evolving job market, landing your dream role requires more than just a polished resume. *The SMART Interview Playbook* equips you with cutting-edge strategies to ace any interview and stand out in the competitive landscape of 2025 and beyond.

From mastering virtual interview dynamics to crafting compelling narratives that resonate with hiring managers, this book offers actionable insights, proven frameworks, and practical exercises tailored for modern professionals. Whether you're a recent graduate or a seasoned professional, this playbook will transform the way you prepare for and approach interviews, giving you the confidence and tools to secure the job you deserve.

Get ready to unlock your potential, master the art of self-presentation, and take charge of your career trajectory with *The SMART Interview Playbook*. Your future starts here!

Why Read this Book

Stay Ahead of the Curve: The job market is evolving rapidly, with new technologies and hiring trends shaping the way employers assess candidates. This book provides up-to-date strategies to help you adapt and excel in this dynamic landscape.

Practical, Actionable Insights: Forget generic advice. This playbook offers step-by-step techniques, real-world examples, and interactive exercises to ensure you're fully prepared for every stage of the interview process.

Master Virtual and In-Person Interviews: With remote work and hybrid models becoming the norm, you'll learn how to shine in both virtual and face-to-face settings, ensuring you're versatile and confident no matter the format.

Stand Out from the Competition: Learn how to craft memorable answers, build rapport with interviewers, and communicate your unique value effectively to leave a lasting impression.

Future-Proof Your Career: Whether you're applying for your first job, making a career pivot, or aiming for a leadership role, this book provides lifelong skills to navigate interviews and secure opportunities in any industry.

The SMART Interview Playbook isn't just a guide—it's your ultimate career companion for thriving in 2025 and beyond.

Target Audience

Job Seekers at All Levels: Whether you're a recent graduate looking for your first role, a mid-career professional seeking a change, or an executive aiming for leadership positions, this book provides tailored strategies to help you succeed.

Career Changers: If you're transitioning to a new industry or role, this playbook equips you with tools to highlight transferable skills and navigate unfamiliar interview processes confidently.

Remote and Hybrid Job Seekers: For those applying to roles in remote or hybrid work environments, this book offers specific insights into mastering virtual interviews and showcasing adaptability in evolving workplaces.

Professionals in Competitive Industries: Individuals in fast-paced, high-demand fields like tech, finance, healthcare, or creative industries can gain a competitive edge with the advanced techniques outlined in this book.

Students and Graduates: Aspiring professionals entering the workforce will find actionable advice to stand out, even with limited experience, and land internships or entry-level roles.

Recruiters and Career Coaches: Those guiding others through the interview process can use this book as a resource for up-to-date methods and best practices in candidate preparation.

If you're ready to elevate your interview skills, stand out in a competitive job market, and secure the career of your dreams, *The SMART Interview Playbook* is written for you.

Prologue: The Interview Revolution

Imagine this: It's 2025, and you've just received an invitation for an interview at your dream company. You've spent hours scrolling through advice blogs, watching videos, and rehearsing answers. But as you step into the interview—whether virtual or in person—you realize the old playbook no longer applies. The questions feel more nuanced, the expectations higher, and the stakes even greater.

The world of interviews has changed. Today's hiring process isn't just about qualifications; it's about connection, adaptability, and a deep understanding of how to market yourself as the best fit for the role. Technology has reshaped the landscape, with AI-driven assessments, virtual reality onboarding, and algorithms analyzing your responses. But beneath all the advancements lies one unchanging truth: success hinges on how well you tell your story.

This book is your guide to thriving in this new era. *The SMART Interview Playbook* isn't just about answering questions—it's about anticipating them. It's about mastering the art of strategic storytelling, leveraging data to understand what employers want, and presenting yourself as the solution they're searching for.

Over the years, I've seen countless individuals struggle to translate their potential into performance during interviews. Some were overwhelmed by nerves, others were blindsided by unexpected questions, and many simply didn't know how to articulate their value. I wrote this book to bridge that gap—to provide you with a toolkit that empowers you to walk into any interview with confidence and clarity.

As you turn these pages, you'll find actionable strategies, relatable examples, and exercises designed to sharpen your skills. This isn't just a book; it's a blueprint for success. Together, we'll redefine how you approach interviews, transforming them from intimidating hurdles into exciting opportunities to showcase the best version of yourself.

Your future starts now. Let's make sure you're ready.

Chapter 1: Unlocking the SMART Interview Secret: Proven Strategies That Work

In today's fast-paced world, where technological advancements and global competition redefine job markets, mastering the art of the interview has never been more crucial. The stakes are higher, the competition fiercer, and the expectations from candidates more rigorous than ever. Yet, amidst this complexity, one guiding framework has emerged as a game-changer: **The SMART Interview Method**. This chapter unveils how this innovative approach empowers candidates to excel, delivering actionable strategies that align with the demands of 2025 and beyond.

The Interview Landscape: A New Era of Expectations

Gone are the days when a firm handshake and a polished résumé could secure your dream job. Today, employers look for **multidimensional candidates** who combine technical expertise, emotional intelligence, adaptability, and a capacity to learn. Interviews are no longer just about answering questions; they're about **telling your story**, demonstrating your value, and proving you can drive results in an unpredictable world.

The SMART Interview Method addresses this challenge head-on. It is a systematic, proven framework designed to help candidates structure their responses, highlight their strengths, and leave a lasting impression. But before diving into the specifics, let's explore why such a method is indispensable in today's competitive job market.

The Problem with Traditional Interview Preparation

Most job seekers approach interviews with outdated techniques. Memorizing generic answers to predictable questions such as "Tell me about yourself" or "What are your strengths and weaknesses?" is no longer sufficient. Interviewers are now trained to dig deeper, assessing not only **what you say** but also **how you think** and **how well you adapt** to high-pressure situations.

Traditional preparation often overlooks the importance of:

Customization: Tailoring answers to the specific company, role, and industry.
Engagement: Creating an interactive, two-way dialogue that keeps the interviewer intrigued.
Metrics: Using quantifiable evidence to back up claims about achievements.

This is where the SMART method becomes transformative.

What is the SMART Interview Method?

The SMART method borrows from the goal-setting acronym—Specific, Measurable, Achievable, Relevant, and Time-bound—but adapts it specifically for interview success. Let's break it down:

Specific: Every answer should directly address the question while staying relevant to the role.

Measurable: Use data, figures, or quantifiable outcomes to validate your accomplishments.

Achievable: Showcase realistic solutions and achievements that demonstrate your resourcefulness.

Relevant: Align your responses with the company's mission, values, and goals.

Time-bound: Highlight projects or tasks within a clear timeline to convey efficiency.

Each component ensures your responses are concise, impactful, and memorable. By mastering this structure, you transform your interview performance into a compelling narrative that sets you apart.

Why the SMART Method Works

What makes the SMART method revolutionary is its emphasis on **storytelling and substance**. In 2025, hiring managers are inundated with candidates who can claim to be "team players" or "results-driven." What distinguishes you is your ability to:

Provide context: Why was the task important?

Show impact: What were the tangible outcomes of your actions?

Engage emotionally: How did your contribution improve the team, client, or company?

The SMART approach integrates these elements seamlessly, ensuring you deliver a standout performance every time.

Preparing for Success with SMART

Preparation is the cornerstone of a successful interview, and the SMART method simplifies this process. Follow these key steps to integrate the framework into your preparation strategy:

1. Research Extensively

Start by gathering in-depth information about the company, the industry, and the specific role you're applying for. Understand their challenges, goals, and culture.

Example: If the company is a tech startup expanding into international markets, tailor your responses to showcase your ability to work in cross-cultural teams or scale operations globally.

2. Analyze the Job Description

Identify the top 3–5 competencies the role demands. Craft SMART-based examples that demonstrate your expertise in these areas.

Example: If leadership is a key requirement, prepare a SMART answer highlighting a project where you successfully led a team to achieve measurable results under a tight deadline.

3. Practice with STAR + SMART

While STAR (Situation, Task, Action, Result) provides a storytelling foundation, integrating SMART ensures your answers are targeted and data-driven.

Example: When describing a past success, use STAR to outline the narrative and SMART to add depth and precision.

4. Leverage Metrics

Quantifiable data is your best ally. Interviewers are more likely to remember specifics like "increased sales by 35%" or "reduced processing time by 50%" than vague achievements.

5. Prepare SMART Follow-Up Questions

Interviews are dialogues, not monologues. Prepare thoughtful questions that demonstrate your understanding of the company's challenges and your eagerness to contribute.

Example: "How does the team measure success in this role, and what SMART goals would you recommend for the first six months?"

Examples of SMART Answers

Here's how to transform generic answers into SMART responses:

Question: "Tell me about a time you improved a process at work."

Generic Answer: "I streamlined our onboarding process, and it worked really well."

SMART Answer:

Situation: "Our onboarding process was taking 3 months, causing delays in new hires becoming fully productive."

Task: "My goal was to reduce this time by 50% without compromising training quality."

Action: "I analyzed bottlenecks, automated repetitive tasks, and introduced a mentorship program."

Result: "We cut onboarding time to 6 weeks, saving the company $50,000 annually in training costs while improving employee satisfaction scores by 20%."

Notice how the SMART answer is specific, measurable, and outcome-focused, leaving a lasting impression on the interviewer.

Building Confidence: Practice Makes Perfect

Even the most well-prepared answers can falter without practice. Use the following techniques to refine your SMART interview skills:

Mock Interviews: Practice with a mentor or friend, requesting feedback on clarity and conciseness.

Video Recording: Record your responses to evaluate your tone, body language, and pacing.

Iterative Refinement: Continuously improve your examples based on feedback.

The key is to make your delivery feel natural and confident while staying aligned with the SMART framework.

The Final Ingredient: Authenticity

As you implement the SMART method, remember this: authenticity is non-negotiable. Employers value candidates who are not only prepared but also genuine. Avoid over-polishing your answers to the point where they sound rehearsed. Instead, let your passion, personality, and enthusiasm shine through.

The SMART Interview Method isn't just a strategy—it's a transformative approach that empowers you to own the narrative, showcase your unique strengths, and stand out in an increasingly competitive job market. By blending preparation, storytelling, and data-driven insights, you can unlock the secret to interview success and take the next step toward your dream career.

As you progress through this book, you'll dive deeper into real-world examples, actionable tips, and advanced techniques to refine your interview mastery. Get ready to turn interviews from daunting challenges into opportunities to shine. The SMART method is your secret weapon—use it wisely.

The SMART Framework: A Proven Strategy for Mastering Modern Interviews

In the ever-evolving world of work, where competition is fierce and opportunities are vast, standing out in an interview requires more than a polished résumé or a charming personality. Modern employers demand clarity, confidence, and evidence of your value—qualities that often remain elusive without a structured approach. This is where the **SMART framework** becomes a game-changer. Adapted from its original use in goal setting, the SMART framework (Specific, Measurable, Achievable, Relevant, Time-bound) is a powerful tool to craft compelling interview responses that captivate employers and leave a lasting impression.

Let's navigate now the SMART framework in detail, demonstrating how it transforms the way candidates prepare for and navigate interviews. By the end, you'll have actionable insights and practical examples to incorporate SMART into your interview strategy, ensuring that you not only meet but exceed employer expectations.

The Evolution of Interviewing

To appreciate the power of the SMART framework, it's essential to understand how interviews have evolved. Traditional interviews focused on a candidate's ability to articulate skills and experiences. Today, interviews are multidimensional evaluations, assessing not just qualifications but also adaptability, problem-solving abilities, and cultural fit.

Employers now use behavioral and situational questions to dig deeper. They want to know not just **what** you've accomplished, but also **how** you achieved it and **why** it matters. This shift has made generic answers obsolete. The need for a structured approach like SMART has never been greater.

What is the SMART Framework?

The SMART framework helps structure answers that are clear, concise, and compelling. Let's break down each component and its relevance in interviews:

1. Specific

Your answers must be precise, directly addressing the question while avoiding vagueness. Specificity demonstrates focus and preparation.

Example: Instead of saying, "I improved team efficiency," say, "I implemented a project management system that reduced task duplication and improved team efficiency by 25%."

2. Measurable

Quantifying your achievements adds credibility and makes your impact tangible. Numbers, percentages, or concrete outcomes resonate more than abstract claims.

Example: "I increased customer satisfaction" becomes "I increased customer satisfaction scores by 15% in six months through improved service protocols."

3. Achievable

Your examples should reflect realistic accomplishments that showcase your resourcefulness and problem-solving skills. Avoid exaggerations or unattainable feats.

Example: Claiming to triple company revenue single-handedly might raise eyebrows, but detailing how you contributed to a 20% increase in revenue by optimizing marketing strategies is both credible and impressive.

4. Relevant

Tailoring your answers to the specific role and company demonstrates that you've done your homework. Relevance connects your experience to the employer's needs and goals.

Example: For a marketing role, emphasize campaign successes rather than unrelated administrative tasks.

5. Time-bound

Including timelines in your responses highlights your efficiency and ability to deliver results within deadlines. It adds a sense of urgency and achievement.

Example: Instead of saying, "I led a successful project," specify, "I led a project that delivered a new product to market within three months, meeting all deadlines and budget constraints."

Why the SMART Framework Works

In interviews, it's easy to ramble or provide disjointed answers under pressure. SMART provides a clear structure, ensuring your responses are focused, memorable, and impactful. It appeals to interviewers for three key reasons:

Clarity: SMART answers eliminate ambiguity, making it easy for interviewers to understand your contributions.

Credibility: Measurable outcomes lend authenticity and weight to your claims.

Engagement: Specific, relevant examples keep the conversation dynamic and interesting.

Employers are often overwhelmed with generic responses. By using SMART, you cut through the noise and position yourself as a thoughtful, results-oriented professional.

Applying SMART to Common Interview Questions

Let's explore how the SMART framework elevates responses to typical interview questions.

1. "Tell me about a time you solved a problem at work."

Generic Answer: "There was an issue with communication in my team, so I worked on improving it, and things got better."

SMART Answer:

Specific: "In my previous role, communication breakdowns between the sales and operations teams were causing delivery delays."

Measurable: "These delays impacted over 20% of orders, leading to a 10% decline in customer satisfaction."

Achievable: "I introduced a shared project management platform and weekly inter-departmental meetings to improve coordination."

Relevant: "This aligned with the company's goal of improving customer retention."

Time-bound: "Within three months, on-time deliveries increased by 30%, and customer satisfaction scores rose by 12%."

This answer paints a vivid picture of the candidate's problem-solving abilities while quantifying their impact.

2. "Why should we hire you?"

Generic Answer: "I'm a hardworking, dedicated professional who always delivers results."

SMART Answer:

Specific: "In my current role as a digital marketing manager, I specialize in optimizing online campaigns for e-commerce businesses."

Measurable: "For example, I increased web traffic by 40% and reduced customer acquisition costs by 25% over six months."

Achievable: "These results were achieved by implementing data-driven strategies and A/B testing for targeted ads."

Relevant: "Given your company's focus on expanding its online presence, my skills directly align with your objectives."

Time-bound: "I am confident I can deliver similar results within the first quarter of joining your team."

This response clearly articulates the candidate's value proposition in relation to the company's needs.

3. "What's your greatest professional achievement?"

Generic Answer: "I helped my company grow revenue."

SMART Answer:

Specific: "At my last company, I noticed we were missing growth opportunities in untapped regional markets."

Measurable: "I launched a regional sales strategy that contributed to a $1.5 million revenue increase within 12 months."

Achievable: "This involved hiring and training five regional sales reps and developing a customized marketing plan for each market."

Relevant: "This approach aligned with the company's broader goal of market diversification."

Time-bound: "The strategy was fully implemented within six months, and the revenue impact was seen within the year."

This response combines storytelling with metrics, making it both engaging and persuasive.

How to Prepare SMART Answers

The SMART framework works best with preparation. Here's a step-by-step process to craft responses:

Step 1: Analyze the Job Description

Identify the key competencies the employer values. These might include leadership, problem-solving, or technical expertise. Your SMART answers should address these areas directly.

Step 2: Choose Relevant Examples

Think of situations where you've demonstrated these competencies. Ensure your examples are specific, measurable, and relevant to the role.

Step 3: Practice the Framework

Use the SMART structure to draft and refine your responses. Practice until they feel natural and conversational, not rehearsed.

Step 4: Anticipate Follow-Up Questions

SMART answers often invite deeper inquiries. Be prepared to elaborate on your approach, challenges, or lessons learned.

Adapting SMART to Different Interview Types

The SMART framework is versatile and works across various interview formats, including:

1. Behavioral Interviews

When asked to provide examples of past experiences, SMART ensures your answers are well-organized and impactful.

2. Panel Interviews

SMART answers help you maintain clarity and confidence, even when addressing multiple interviewers.

3. Virtual Interviews

In remote settings, where non-verbal cues are limited, SMART answers compensate by providing substance and focus.

Beyond the Interview: Using SMART for Career Growth

The beauty of the SMART framework is its adaptability. Beyond interviews, it's a valuable tool for setting career goals, crafting performance reviews, and even negotiating promotions.

For example:

Career Goal: "I aim to increase my technical certifications by completing three relevant courses within the next 12 months."

Performance Review: "In the past year, I've reduced customer response time by 20%, aligning with our goal of improving client satisfaction."

By mastering SMART, you equip yourself with a lifelong strategy for professional success.

The SMART framework isn't just an interview strategy—it's a mindset. In a world where employers seek clarity, results, and relevance, SMART empowers you to meet those expectations with confidence. By structuring your responses around Specificity, Measurability, Achievability, Relevance, and Timeliness, you stand out as a candidate who understands not only the job but also how to deliver value.

As you move forward, remember that interviews are opportunities to showcase your potential. With SMART as your guide, you're not just answering questions—you're telling a story that resonates, inspires, and leaves no doubt that you're the right choice. Let this framework become your secret weapon, transforming every interview into a stepping stone toward your dream career.

Chapter 2: The Art of Answering with Impact: Winning Over Interviewers with Memorable Responses

Why Memorable Answers Matter

In the high-stakes world of interviews, your answers aren't just words; they're your personal brand in action. Crafting memorable responses isn't just about saying the right thing—it's about creating an emotional connection that lingers long after the conversation ends. When interviewers recall your answers with clarity, you become the candidate who stands out in a sea of sameness.

Memorability doesn't mean rehearsing to perfection. It's about authenticity, relevance, and precision. A memorable response transforms a generic answer into a powerful narrative—one that positions you as confident, capable, and irreplaceable.

The SMART Approach to Answering Questions

To make your responses impactful, adopt the SMART framework:

Specific: Provide concrete examples to showcase your experience and skills.

Measurable: Use metrics to highlight achievements and results.

Authentic: Reflect your true self while aligning with the role's demands.

Relevant: Tailor your response to the job and the company's values.

Tactful: Strike a balance between confidence and humility.

Turning Challenges into Triumphs: The STAR+L Method

One of the most effective ways to structure memorable answers is by using the STAR method (Situation, Task, Action, Result). Let's enhance it with an additional layer—Learning (STAR+L)—to show growth and adaptability. Here's how it works:

Situation: Set the stage by briefly explaining the context.

Task: Describe the challenge or responsibility you faced.

Action: Share what you did to address the challenge, focusing on your role.

Result: Highlight the outcome, emphasizing metrics if possible.

Learning: Reflect on what the experience taught you and how it prepared you for future challenges.

Example STAR+L Answer

Question: *"Tell me about a time you overcame a significant challenge at work."*

Situation: "In my previous role as a marketing specialist, our team faced an unexpected budget cut midway through a critical campaign."

Task: "My responsibility was to revise the campaign strategy to achieve our goals despite the financial constraints."

Action: "I analyzed past campaign data to identify the highest-impact channels and negotiated with vendors to lower costs. Additionally, I leveraged free social media tools to amplify reach."

Result: "The campaign achieved 120% of its target with 40% less budget, earning recognition from senior management."

Learning: "This experience taught me the value of resourcefulness and adaptability. It reinforced the importance of data-driven decisions and creative problem-solving."

Crafting the Perfect Elevator Pitch

At some point in your interview, you'll likely be asked the infamous question: *"Tell me about yourself."* This isn't just a casual icebreaker; it's your golden opportunity to create a powerful first impression.

The 3-Part Structure for an Elevator Pitch

Introduction: Briefly describe your professional background.

Highlight: Showcase a key achievement or skill that aligns with the role.

Connection: Explain why you're excited about this opportunity.

Example Elevator Pitch

"I've spent the last five years as a software engineer specializing in developing scalable e-commerce platforms. In my previous role, I led a team that improved website load times by 40%, resulting in a 25% increase in sales. I'm passionate about using technology to enhance user experiences, and I'm thrilled at the prospect of bringing my skills to a forward-thinking company like yours."

How to Handle Tricky Questions

Interviewers often throw curveballs to test your critical thinking, emotional intelligence, or ability to handle pressure. Here's how to navigate common challenging questions:

1. "What's Your Greatest Weakness?"

Avoid clichés like *"I'm a perfectionist."* Instead, choose a genuine weakness you've actively worked to improve.

Response:

"In the past, I struggled with delegating tasks because I wanted to ensure everything was perfect. However, I've since learned the importance of trust and team collaboration. I now focus on empowering my team and providing support where needed, which has enhanced our overall productivity."

2. "Why Should We Hire You?"

This is your chance to connect your unique skills with the company's needs.

Response:

"Your company's focus on sustainability resonates deeply with me. With my experience in supply chain optimization and a proven track record of reducing logistics costs by 30%, I'm confident I can contribute to your mission of creating eco-friendly solutions while driving operational efficiency."

Building Connection Through Personalization

Interviewers are more likely to remember candidates who show genuine interest in their company. Research the organization thoroughly and weave your findings into your answers. Mentioning specific projects, values, or milestones demonstrates preparation and enthusiasm.

Example Response with Personalization

Question: *"Why do you want to work here?"*

"I admire your company's recent commitment to renewable energy initiatives, particularly the launch of your solar panel program. My background in project management, coupled with my passion for sustainable innovation, makes me excited to contribute to such impactful work."

The Role of Storytelling in Interviews

Stories are memorable because they evoke emotions and engage the listener. By framing your answers as narratives, you'll leave a lasting impression.

Elements of a Compelling Story

Conflict: Highlight the challenge or problem you faced.

Resolution: Explain your approach and actions.

Impact: Showcase the results and what it meant for you or your team.

Example Story

Question: *"Can you tell me about a time you led a team?"*

"When our department was tasked with launching a new product in three months, we faced resistance from cross-functional teams due to tight deadlines. I initiated weekly check-ins to foster collaboration and addressed concerns proactively. By uniting the teams under a shared vision, we launched on time and exceeded sales targets by 15%. This experience reinforced my belief in the power of communication and teamwork."

The Power of Follow-Up Questions

A truly impactful answer often leads to a deeper conversation. Encourage this by concluding your response with an insightful remark or a question.

Example

Response:

"This project taught me the importance of aligning team goals with organizational priorities. Have you found that alignment to be a challenge in this role?"

This technique positions you as an engaged and thoughtful candidate while gaining valuable insights into the company.

Practicing for Perfection

The key to answering with impact lies in preparation. Here are some tips for effective practice:

Record Yourself: Listen for clarity, tone, and confidence.

Mock Interviews: Practice with a friend or mentor.

Feedback Loop: Seek constructive criticism to refine your delivery.

Mastering the art of answering with impact is about more than rehearsing responses—it's about showcasing your authentic self in a way that resonates with interviewers. By combining structure, personalization, and storytelling, you'll leave an indelible mark that makes you the candidate they can't forget.

A Deep Dive into Crafting Impactful Answers Using SMART Techniques and Storytelling

Interviewing is an art as much as it is a skill. While technical qualifications and experience get your foot in the door, the ability to communicate effectively determines whether you make it across the threshold. Crafting impactful answers, particularly in high-stakes situations, requires thoughtful preparation, deliberate structure, and the use of storytelling techniques that resonate.

Let's explore the **three principal challenges** candidates face when crafting impactful answers and how the **SMART framework** combined with storytelling can overcome them.

Challenge 1: Balancing Specificity and Brevity

One of the most common challenges in interviews is striking the right balance between providing enough detail to demonstrate competence and keeping responses concise to maintain the interviewer's attention. Candidates often fall into one of two traps:

Over-explaining: Giving too much background or excessive detail, which causes the interviewer to lose focus.

Under-explaining: Providing vague or generic responses that fail to convey real value or insight.

Solution: SMART Techniques for Precision

The SMART framework—Specific, Measurable, Authentic, Relevant, and Tactful—serves as a blueprint to craft answers that are both concise and compelling.

Specific: Get straight to the point by focusing on what the interviewer needs to know. Avoid unnecessary jargon or irrelevant tangents.

Measurable: Incorporate data or metrics to quantify your contributions, making your achievements tangible.

Authentic: Be honest and personal in your answers, reflecting your unique experiences.

Relevant: Tailor your response to align with the job role and company goals.

Tactful: Choose words that convey confidence without arrogance, and adapt your tone to suit the situation.

Example: Using SMART to Answer "Tell Me About a Challenge You Overcame"

Generic Response:

"I faced a tough project once, but I worked hard, and everything turned out fine."

SMART Response:

"In my previous role as a logistics coordinator, we encountered a sudden supply chain disruption due to a key vendor shutting down. My responsibility was to identify alternative suppliers without impacting delivery schedules. I immediately leveraged our database to identify three potential replacements and negotiated expedited contracts. As a result, we avoided a delay in shipments and maintained a 98% on-time delivery rate, even during the disruption. This experience reinforced my ability to adapt quickly and maintain operational efficiency under pressure."

Why This Works

Specific: Describes the exact challenge (vendor shutdown).

Measurable: Quantifies the outcome (98% on-time delivery rate).

Authentic: Reflects personal initiative and problem-solving.

Relevant: Shows skills applicable to the role.

Tactful: Demonstrates confidence in solving high-pressure issues.

Challenge 2: Making Answers Memorable

With dozens of candidates competing for the same position, interviewers often hear similar responses. This makes it difficult for any one answer to stand out. The key to being remembered is **storytelling**—an approach that transforms dry facts into engaging narratives.

Solution: Crafting Stories Using the STAR+L Model

The STAR+L method (Situation, Task, Action, Result + Learning) elevates storytelling by adding a personal growth element. This structure ensures your answers are both impactful and memorable.

Situation: Start with a brief context.

Task: Outline the specific responsibility or challenge you faced.

Action: Explain the steps you took to address the challenge, highlighting your role.

Result: Share the measurable outcomes of your actions.

Learning: Reflect on the experience and what it taught you, showcasing your adaptability and growth.

Example: Answering "Describe a Time You Improved a Process" Using STAR+L

Storytelling Response:

"When I joined my previous company, our invoicing process was entirely manual, leading to frequent delays and errors. My task was to streamline this process to improve efficiency. I researched and implemented an automated invoicing system, trained the team, and created detailed user manuals. As a result, we reduced invoice errors by 80% and cut processing time from 5 days to 1. This experience taught me the importance of leveraging technology to solve operational challenges and strengthened my ability to lead organizational change."

Why Storytelling Works

Engages Emotions: Stories evoke feelings, making your answers more relatable and human.

Creates Visual Imagery: A well-crafted narrative helps interviewers visualize your role and impact.

Demonstrates Depth: Storytelling reveals not just what you've done but also how you think and grow.

Challenge 3: Handling Ambiguous or Unexpected Questions

Ambiguity is a deliberate tool interviewers use to assess a candidate's critical thinking, creativity, and composure under pressure. Questions like *"If you were an animal, what would you be?"* or *"How do you deal with failure?"* are designed to push you out of your comfort zone.

Solution: Combining SMART and Storytelling for Ambiguity

Pause and Reflect: Take a moment to understand the intent behind the question.

Structure Your Answer: Use SMART to create a concise response.

Add a Narrative: Share a story that aligns with your answer, showcasing your ability to think critically and act effectively.

Example: Answering "Tell Me About a Failure You've Had"

SMART + Storytelling Response:

"During a product launch, I underestimated the time required for quality assurance testing. As a result, the launch was delayed by two weeks, which impacted the marketing timeline. To address this, I conducted a post-mortem with the team to identify where our planning fell short. I then implemented a more robust project timeline system that factored in additional testing periods. This new approach reduced delays in subsequent launches by 25%. While the initial

failure was challenging, it taught me the importance of meticulous planning and proactive risk management."

Why This Approach Works
  SMART Elements:
  Specific: Clearly defines the failure (delayed product launch).
  Measurable: Quantifies the improvement (25% fewer delays).
  Authentic: Honestly acknowledges a mistake.
  Relevant: Demonstrates transferable skills like project management.
  Tactful: Emphasizes learning over the failure itself.
  Storytelling Elements:
  Conflict: A clear challenge (delayed timeline).
  Resolution: Proactive actions taken to solve the issue.
  Impact: Tangible results that benefit future projects.

Bringing It All Together: The Triple Impact Strategy
  Combining **SMART techniques** with **storytelling** addresses all three challenges, ensuring your answers are:
  Clear and Concise: You provide just the right amount of detail to keep the interviewer engaged.
  Engaging and Memorable: You leave a lasting impression through narrative-driven responses.
  Adaptable: You can handle ambiguity and tailor your answers to diverse scenarios.

Practice Exercise: Applying the Triple Impact Strategy
  Choose three common interview questions and craft your answers using SMART and storytelling techniques. Practice delivering them aloud to refine your tone, pacing, and confidence.
  Question: *"Why do you want to work here?"*
  SMART Key Points: Specific role alignment, measurable enthusiasm, authentic career goals, relevance to company values, tactful tone.
  Storytelling Example: Share a personal anecdote that connects your career journey to the company's mission.

Question: *"Where do you see yourself in 5 years?"*

SMART Key Points: Specific career aspirations, measurable milestones, authentic passion, relevance to the company's growth, tactful ambition.

Storytelling Example: Describe a vision that aligns personal growth with the company's goals.

Question: *"How do you handle conflict in the workplace?"*

SMART Key Points: Specific conflict scenario, measurable resolution, authentic approach, relevance to teamwork skills, tactful communication.

Storytelling Example: Narrate a situation where you resolved a team conflict, emphasizing the positive outcome.

Crafting impactful answers is a skill that improves with preparation and practice. By combining the SMART framework and storytelling techniques, you'll not only excel in interviews but also leave a lasting impression that sets you apart.

Remember, it's not just about answering questions—it's about telling your story in a way that makes interviewers believe you're the perfect fit for their team.

Challenge	Description	Solution	Key Example	Impact
1. Balancing Specificity and Brevity	Difficulty in providing detailed answers without overloading or underwhelming the interviewer.	Use the SMART framework: Specific, Measurable, Authentic, Relevant, Tactful.	Example: Answering "Tell me about a challenge you overcame" using SMART to quantify outcomes and focus on relevance.	Clear, concise answers that demonstrate value and competence effectively.
2. Making Answers Memorable	Generic answers fail to leave a lasting impression on interviewers.	Leverage the STAR+L model (Situation, Task, Action, Result + Learning) to craft compelling, structured stories.	Example: Answering "Describe a time you improved a process" with STAR+L, emphasizing tangible outcomes and growth.	Memorable responses that resonate with interviewers through engaging narratives.
3. Handling Ambiguous Questions	Ambiguous or unexpected questions test critical thinking and adaptability.	Combine SMART techniques and storytelling to create structured, reflective answers.	Example: Answering "Tell me about a failure" by explaining the mistake, corrective actions, and measurable results.	Adaptability and composure are demonstrated effectively, even in challenging scenarios.

Chapter 3: Beyond the Résumé: Building Your Personal Brand to Stand Out in 2025 and Beyond

Introduction: Why Your Résumé Is No Longer Enough

In 2025, recruiters aren't just skimming résumés—they're searching your name on LinkedIn, Instagram, and even Google. They want more than a list of jobs and degrees. They want a story. A résumé tells where you've been; your personal brand shows who you are and where you're going.

Let's face it: in today's digital-first world, your personal brand isn't optional. It's your unique promise of value, a compelling narrative that distinguishes you from the competition. Think of it as your professional "vibe" that stays with people long after you've left the room—or the Zoom call.

Let me ask you something right now:

When was the last time you Googled yourself? What came up?

If it wasn't what you'd like a potential employer or client to see, this chapter will change that.

What Is a Personal Brand?

Your personal brand is a mix of what people think, feel, and say about you when you're not in the room. It's built through every interaction—online or offline—and it's more crucial than ever in 2025, a time when AI-powered algorithms prioritize human stories over generic résumés. A strong personal brand gives you:

Visibility: Recruiters and collaborators find you easily.

Credibility: Your expertise is evident across platforms.

Opportunities: The right doors open without you knocking.

Step 1: Define Your Brand

Who Are You? The Core Question

Think about what makes you *you*. Here's a quick exercise:

33

Grab a pen or open a notes app and answer these questions:

What are three words people often use to describe you?

What are your top strengths or skills?

What problems are you passionate about solving?

Now, take a moment to reflect. Are the words that came to mind the same ones you'd *like* to be associated with? If not, this is your starting point to recalibrate.

Interactive moment:

Close your eyes and imagine your dream job or opportunity. What kind of person do they want to hire? Are you that person?

Step 2: Tell Your Story Authentically

The Power of Storytelling

Humans connect with stories, not bullet points. Your story should answer three key questions:

Who are you?

What do you stand for?

Why should people care?

Example:

Let's say you're a software engineer passionate about sustainability.

Résumé version: "Developed code for renewable energy platforms."

Personal brand version: "As a coder committed to a greener planet, I create digital solutions that empower businesses to cut carbon footprints."

Notice the difference? One lists facts; the other inspires.

Step 3: Build Your Online Presence

Own Your Digital Real Estate

In 2025, your online presence is your storefront. Here's where to focus:

LinkedIn: Optimize your headline with keywords. For example:

"Product Manager | Driving Innovation in EdTech | Growth Strategist"

Add a professional photo (smiling, confident, and approachable).

Use the "Featured" section to showcase articles, projects, or videos that align with your brand.

Social Media: Platforms like Instagram and Twitter are now tools for thought leadership. Share meaningful content related to your industry or passions.

Personal Website: If you can, create a website. A simple one-page portfolio with your bio, work samples, and contact info can set you apart.

Quick question for you:

If someone visited your LinkedIn right now, would they know what you stand for in under 10 seconds? If not, it's time to tweak.

Step 4: Network Like a Pro

Authentic Networking

Gone are the days of awkward handshakes and exchanging business cards. Networking in 2025 is about forming genuine connections, both online and offline.

Pro Tips:

Engage on LinkedIn: Comment thoughtfully on industry posts. Don't just "like" them—share your insights.

Attend Virtual Events: They're here to stay. Choose conferences, webinars, or panels where you can learn *and* make connections.

Be the Giver: Offer value first. Share resources, introduce people, or lend your expertise.

Step 5: The Three Cs of Personal Branding

Clarity: Be crystal clear about your message.

Consistency: Maintain your brand across platforms.

Confidence: Own your story.

Clarity in Action

Imagine you're an aspiring marketing manager. Your clarity statement could be:

"I help brands tell compelling stories that drive audience engagement and sales."

Real Talk: Overcoming Impostor Syndrome

Have you ever felt like you're not "good enough" to build a personal brand?

Newsflash: Everyone feels this way at some point—even the most accomplished professionals.

Here's how to push past it:

Focus on progress, not perfection.

Remember, your voice is unique. No one else has *your* experiences or insights.

Question for you:

What's one skill or achievement you've downplayed that deserves more spotlight? Write it down now and commit to sharing it this week.

Case Study: The Rise of Emma Jones

Emma was a graphic designer who struggled to land clients because her portfolio was scattered. She decided to rebrand herself as "The Minimalist Designer," specializing in sleek, modern designs for tech startups.

Here's what Emma did:

Defined her brand: Minimalism + technology.

Updated her profiles: Her LinkedIn banner read: "Helping tech startups design with clarity and impact."

Showcased thought leadership: She posted "before-and-after" design transformations with insights.

Within six months, Emma landed a dream client and tripled her income.

Your turn:

What niche or unique angle could you own?

Step 6: Monitor Your Brand

Your personal brand isn't static. It evolves as you grow. Regularly audit your online presence to ensure it aligns with your goals.

DIY Brand Audit Checklist:

Google your name.

Review your LinkedIn and other platforms.

Ask three trusted colleagues: "What's the first thing that comes to mind when you think of me professionally?"

In 2025, the strongest candidates won't just have polished résumés—they'll have powerful personal brands. Remember, you're the CEO of *You Inc.* Start today, and by the time the opportunities roll in, you'll be ready.

Last question for you:

What's one action you'll take today to elevate your personal brand?

Write it down. Then take that step. Your future self will thank you.

Positioning Yourself as the Ideal Candidate in a Competitive Job Market

In today's job market, competition isn't just fierce—it's unrelenting. With advancements in AI, globalization, and hybrid work structures, employers have access to a deeper, more diverse talent pool than ever before. To stand out, you need to be more than just qualified—you need to be unforgettable.

This chapter will guide you through crafting a unique professional narrative, honing the skills that matter, and showcasing them strategically so that hiring managers see you as *the* ideal candidate.

The Big Picture: Why Positioning Matters

Think of job hunting like marketing. In marketing, companies differentiate their products to make them irresistible. The same principle applies to you. Positioning yourself as the ideal candidate means aligning your unique skills, experiences, and personality with what a specific employer needs.

Here's a critical truth: **It's not always about being the best; it's about being the best fit.**

Critical Question 1: *Have you researched what "ideal" looks like for the jobs you want?*

If not, that's your first task. It's impossible to position yourself effectively without knowing what employers are truly seeking.

Step 1: Research Deeply and Strategically

To position yourself as the ideal candidate, you must deeply understand the job, the company, and the industry.

Go Beyond Job Descriptions

Most job seekers stop at reading job descriptions. Not you. You're here to dig deeper. Here's how:

Study the Company Culture:
Check LinkedIn posts, Glassdoor reviews, and the company's website.
What values and language stand out? Are they innovative, traditional, or socially driven?

Analyze Current Trends:
What's happening in the industry? Are companies prioritizing sustainability, AI, or employee well-being?

Identify Key Challenges:

Look for pain points the company might be facing (e.g., expansion, digital transformation, or new regulations).

Interactive Exercise:

Write down one major challenge your target company is facing. How could you help solve it?

Step 2: Highlight Relevant Skills and Experiences

Employers today are looking for "plug-and-play" candidates—those who can hit the ground running. Your job is to show how your skills align with their immediate needs.

Core vs. Adaptive Skills

Core Skills: Industry-specific knowledge like data analysis, project management, or coding.

Adaptive Skills: Transferable abilities like leadership, communication, and problem-solving.

To position yourself as ideal:

Tailor your résumé and cover letter to emphasize skills directly tied to the role.

Highlight success stories that showcase measurable impact. Use the **STAR method** (Situation, Task, Action, Result).

Example:

Instead of saying:

"Managed a team of five."

Say:

"Led a cross-functional team of five to deliver a $2M project 10% under budget and two weeks ahead of schedule."

Critical Question 2: *What's one recent success you can frame as a solution to your target employer's needs?*

Step 3: Craft a Compelling Narrative

What's Your Unique Selling Proposition (USP)?

Your USP is the unique blend of skills, experiences, and personality traits that make you the best fit. It's your professional "elevator pitch."

How to Create Your USP:

Identify Strengths: What do you excel at, both technically and personally?

Understand Needs: How do your strengths solve specific employer challenges?

Tell a Story: Combine the two in a concise, memorable way.

Example of a USP:

"I'm a data analyst passionate about using predictive modeling to solve real-world problems. My recent project helped a retail client reduce inventory costs by 20%, and I'd love to bring that expertise to your e-commerce platform."

Step 4: Leverage Digital Tools

In a competitive job market, how you present yourself online can be the deciding factor.

LinkedIn Optimization

Your LinkedIn profile is your professional storefront. Here's how to make it shine:

Headline: Use keywords related to your industry. For example:

"Customer Success Manager | SaaS Growth Specialist | Empowering Clients to Scale"

About Section: Share your USP and career highlights in 3–5 short paragraphs.

Skills Section: Add skills that match the job description.

Social Proof Matters

Ask for recommendations from colleagues or clients that align with your positioning. Nothing says "ideal candidate" like glowing testimonials.

Critical Question 3: *If an employer Googled you, would they see proof of your expertise and values? If not, what's missing?*

Step 5: Master the Art of Interviews

Landing an interview means you're halfway there. Now, it's time to seal the deal.

Prepare to Solve Problems

Hiring managers want solutions. During your interview, position yourself as a problem-solver by:

Researching the Company's Challenges: Be ready to discuss how you can address them.

Sharing Case Studies: Use real examples from your past experience.

Example:

Interviewer: "We're struggling with employee retention in our IT department."

You: "In my last role, I implemented a mentorship program that reduced turnover by 15% in six months. I'd love to bring that initiative here."

Body Language and Confidence

Non-verbal cues are just as important as your words. Smile, make eye contact, and use open gestures to convey confidence.

Step 6: Follow Up Strategically

After an interview, send a personalized thank-you email that:

Reiterates your enthusiasm.

Mentions something specific from the conversation.

Highlights one final reason why you're the ideal candidate.

Example:

"Thank you for the opportunity to discuss how my background in supply chain optimization aligns with your goals. I'm particularly excited about your plans for AI-driven inventory management and would love to contribute to that innovation."

Bonus: The Ideal Candidate Mindset

Finally, positioning yourself as the ideal candidate requires a winning mindset.

Overcome Self-Doubt

Impostor syndrome is real, but here's the truth: Employers are hiring you for your unique skills and perspectives. Own them.

Focus on Fit, Not Perfection

You don't need to check every box on a job description. Highlight what you bring to the table, and show your eagerness to learn the rest.

In today's hyper-competitive job market, positioning yourself as the ideal candidate isn't about luck—it's about strategy. By deeply understanding employer needs, crafting a compelling narrative, and showcasing your value online and offline, you can stand out and win the opportunities you deserve.

Actionable Step: *What's one thing you can do today to align your professional story with your dream job? Write it down and make it happen.*

Your career success starts with the choices you make now. Are you ready to stand out?

Summary Table: Positioning Yourself as the Ideal Candidate

Resources for Success: Apps and Tools to Boost Your Interview Game

So, you've polished your resume, practiced your STAR stories, and finally landed that coveted interview. Congratulations! But here's the thing: the real challenge is just beginning. In today's fast-paced, tech-driven world, your interview preparation isn't complete without leveraging the right apps and tools. Think of them as your personal pit crew, helping you fine-tune every detail before the big race. Ready? Let's explore some interactive, fun, and downright game-changing tools that will make you an interview rockstar!

Step 1: The First Impression Toolkit

We all know the saying: *You never get a second chance to make a first impression.* These tools ensure you shine from the moment you say "hello."

Grammarly

Before you send that thank-you email or fill out an online application, let's get those typos in check. Grammarly isn't just a spellchecker; it's your personal writing coach. Beyond fixing errors, it helps you strike the perfect tone—polished, professional, and confident.

☐ **Pro Tip:** Use the browser extension to review LinkedIn messages or emails. The premium version offers suggestions on word choice and clarity, making sure your communication stands out.

Canva

Why settle for a dull resume or portfolio when Canva can help you create something extraordinary? With its sleek templates and drag-and-drop features, even design rookies can produce visually stunning materials.

☐ **Challenge for You:** Create a personalized cover page for your interview prep notes. It'll get you in the zone and make your practice sessions feel *pro-level*.

Photofeeler

Ever wonder if your LinkedIn photo screams "confident leader" or "awkward selfie-taker"? Photofeeler lets real people vote on your photo's trustworthiness, confidence, and influence levels. You'd be surprised how a small tweak in your headshot can make a big impact.

☐☐ **Activity:** Upload a few options and test the results. Choose the one that scores highest to enhance your professional profile!

Step 2: Sharpen Your Skills with Mock Interview Apps

Practice doesn't just make perfect—it makes confident! These tools allow you to rehearse your responses, get constructive feedback, and walk into the interview room feeling unstoppable.

Big Interview

Big Interview combines video lessons and interactive mock interviews to simulate real-world scenarios. Choose questions tailored to your industry, record your answers, and analyze your performance.

☐ **Interactive Idea:** Record your "Tell me about yourself" answer and replay it. Notice your tone, pace, and body language. Too fast? Too monotone? Refine it until it shines.

Pramp

If practicing alone feels too awkward, Pramp pairs you with a live partner for role-playing. It's perfect for honing behavioral questions or nailing technical challenges. Plus, the feedback is invaluable.

☐ **Fun Twist:** Turn this into a game—who can come up with the most challenging question for the other?

InterviewBuddy

This app connects you with real hiring managers who provide live feedback on your performance. It's like having a secret weapon in your prep arsenal.

☐ **Achievement Unlocked:** Walk away with actionable tips to improve not just your answers but your overall confidence.

Step 3: Master Your Non-Verbal Game

Body language speaks louder than words, and these tools can help you refine what you're silently communicating.

Coach.me

This habit-building app isn't just for fitness or productivity. Use it to develop small, daily habits like maintaining eye contact or improving your posture.

☐ **Micro-Challenge:** Dedicate 5 minutes daily to practicing a confident handshake and natural eye contact. Consistency is key!

Orai

Public speaking nerves? Orai analyzes your voice and provides tips to make it more engaging. From pacing to filler words, this app helps you sound confident and credible.

☐ **Game Mode:** Try reducing "uhs" and "ums" during practice. Set a personal record and aim to beat it before your big day.

Posture Reminder Apps

Apps like Upright or PostureZone can be lifesavers. They send gentle nudges to straighten up, ensuring you appear confident and professional during both in-person and virtual interviews.

☐☐ **Interactive Bonus:** Turn posture correction into a mini-game. Track how long you can maintain an upright position during Zoom calls or prep sessions.

Step 4: Organization is Everything

Preparation without organization is like baking without measuring. These tools ensure you stay on top of every detail, from application to interview follow-up.

Notion

Notion's flexibility makes it the ultimate interview planner. Create a workspace to track companies, job titles, interview dates, and follow-up actions.

☐ **Your Mission:** Design a dashboard with sections like "Key Questions," "STAR Stories," and "Company Insights." Bonus points if you color-code it!

Trello

If lists are your thing, Trello lets you organize tasks into visually appealing boards. Move items from "To Do" to "Done" and feel the sweet satisfaction of progress.

☐ **Friendly Competition:** Reward yourself for every task completed. Ace an interview? Treat yourself to coffee at your favorite café!

Google Calendar

Never miss an interview or prep session again. Use Google Calendar to schedule reminders for mock interviews, application deadlines, and post-interview thank-yous.

☐ **Pro-Tip:** Set a "confidence boost" alert 30 minutes before your interview. Use the time for positive affirmations or a quick power pose!

Step 5: Ace the Digital Interview

Virtual interviews are here to stay, and these tools ensure you shine—even through a screen.

Zoom

A no-brainer, right? But here's the trick: use Zoom to record practice sessions. Analyze everything—from lighting and background to how you articulate answers.

☐ **Interactive Tip:** Test your setup with a friend. Does your face look shadowy? Is the background too distracting? Fix it now, not during the actual interview!

Krisp

Background noise can ruin even the most well-prepared answers. Krisp cancels out barking dogs, honking horns, or noisy neighbors, leaving you to focus on delivering a stellar performance.

☐ **Experiment:** Try Krisp with and without the noise cancellation feature. You'll instantly see (or hear!) the difference.

Mmhmm

Take your virtual presence to the next level with Mmhmm. This app lets you customize your video background or add subtle overlays—like your name or talking points—without appearing over-the-top.

☐ **Creative Task:** Design a virtual "success corner" with inspiring quotes or clean, neutral backgrounds. Keep it polished yet personal.

Step 6: Knowledge is Power

Interviews are a two-way street. These tools help you understand the company, industry, and role inside out.

Glassdoor

From salary insights to company reviews, Glassdoor gives you the inside scoop. Use it to prepare thoughtful questions or gauge what to expect from the interview process.

☐ **Scavenger Hunt:** Find one unique insight about the company to mention during your interview. Bonus points if it sparks a meaningful conversation.

Google Alerts

Set alerts for the company or industry trends. Staying informed shows your enthusiasm and proactive mindset.

☐ **Daily Task:** Review your alerts during breakfast or your commute. Jot down key points in your prep notes.

LinkedIn

Use LinkedIn to research your interviewer's profile, connections, and interests. Finding common ground can make your interview feel more like a conversation than an interrogation.

☐ **Challenge:** Send a personalized connection request after the interview, mentioning a specific detail from your conversation.

Step 7: Post-Interview Excellence

Don't drop the ball after the interview. These tools ensure your follow-up leaves a lasting impression.

ThankView

Want to go the extra mile? ThankView lets you send personalized video thank-you messages. It's memorable, genuine, and shows you care about the opportunity.

☐ **Fun Idea:** Create a 30-second thank-you video template. Keep it professional but let your personality shine!

Boomerang for Gmail

Timing is everything. Boomerang schedules your follow-up emails to land at the perfect moment.

☐ **Pro Tip:** Draft your thank-you email immediately after the interview, but schedule it for the next morning. It shows thoughtfulness and enthusiasm without seeming overeager.

Your Turn: Let's Play!

Now that you have this treasure trove of tools, it's time to *gamify* your interview prep. Here's a challenge for you:

Choose three tools from this list to integrate into your routine today.

Set a goal for each one—like recording a flawless "Tell me about yourself" answer on Big Interview or organizing your interview tracker in Notion.

Share your progress with a friend or mentor.

Think of each app as a player on your team, helping you conquer the interview field one step at a time. And remember: every small win builds momentum for the ultimate prize—your dream job. You've got this!

Chapter 4: "The SMART Method in Action: Essential Q&A Strategies to Shine"

So, you've made it to the pivotal moment of the hiring process—the interview. Congratulations! But let's face it, interviews can be nerve-wracking. The good news? You're armed with the SMART Method: Specific, Measurable, Achievable, Relevant, and Time-bound strategies that will make you a standout candidate. In this chapter, we're going to bring those strategies to life through essential Q&A tactics, interactive exercises, and a dash of storytelling magic to keep things engaging.

By the end, you won't just *know* how to ace an interview—you'll *feel* it.

Let's Warm Up: Breaking the Ice

Imagine this: You're sitting in the lobby, heart racing, palms a little clammy. Suddenly, the interviewer opens the door and smiles. "Welcome! Let's get started."

The first few minutes of any interview are crucial. They set the tone, and they're your chance to establish rapport. Here's where the "S" in SMART—**Specific**—comes into play. Your opening response needs to be clear and tailored.

Common Icebreaker Q:
"Tell me about yourself."

Your SMART Answer:
"Well, I'm a marketing professional with five years of experience specializing in social media strategies that drive measurable growth. For instance, at my last role, I increased engagement by 35% within six months through targeted campaigns. I'm passionate about connecting brands with audiences in meaningful ways, and I'd love to bring that expertise here."

Did you notice how your answer was **specific**, offered **measurable** success, and hinted at **relevant** skills? That's the SMART Method at work.

Interactive Moment: Your Turn!

Take a moment to jot down your answer to "Tell me about yourself." Use these prompts:
What's one key accomplishment you're proud of?

How does it align with the role you're interviewing for?

Can you attach numbers, percentages, or timelines to it?

Now, rehearse it out loud. How does it feel? Confident? Crisp? If not, tweak it until it shines.

Tackling the Tough Ones

Interviews aren't all about warm fuzzies. Let's dive into some tricky questions and how the SMART Method can transform your answers.

The Dreaded Weakness Question

"What's your greatest weakness?"

Many candidates panic here. You, however, will approach this with a SMART spin:

Specific: Pinpoint a skill, not a personality flaw.

Measurable: Mention how you're improving.

Achievable: Show that it's not a dealbreaker.

Relevant: Tie it back to the role.

Time-bound: Highlight recent progress.

Example Answer:

"I used to struggle with delegating tasks because I felt I had to handle everything myself to ensure quality. But over the past year, I've actively worked on this by using project management tools like Asana and scheduling weekly check-ins with my team. As a result, our team's efficiency has improved by 20%, and I've learned to trust the process."

See what happened there? You turned a "weakness" into a strength in progress.

Pop Quiz Time!

Which of these answers is SMART?

Scenario: You're asked, "Where do you see yourself in five years?"

Option A:

"I don't know, just growing and doing my best."

Option B:

"In five years, I see myself in a leadership role, managing a team and driving innovative marketing strategies. I aim to achieve this by continuing to develop my skills in data analysis and campaign management while contributing to a company's long-term growth."

Spoiler alert: It's B. Always be specific and show intention.

Behavioral Questions: Your Time to Shine

Behavioral questions are designed to dig deeper into your past experiences. They often start with "Tell me about a time when…"

The SMART Method here pairs beautifully with the **STAR Method** (Situation, Task, Action, Result). Let's combine the two.

Q: "Tell me about a time you handled a difficult situation at work."

Your Answer:

Situation: "In my previous role, a client threatened to leave due to a misunderstanding about our deliverables."

Task: "I was tasked with resolving the issue and retaining their business."

Action: "I scheduled an immediate call, listened to their concerns, and provided a specific, measurable plan to address the gaps. I also followed up with weekly progress reports to rebuild trust."

Result: "Within a month, their satisfaction score increased from 6 to 9 out of 10, and they renewed their contract for another year."

Notice how every element ties back to SMART principles? The interviewer sees that you're thoughtful, results-driven, and capable of handling pressure.

Play Along: Your STAR Moment

Grab a pen or open a notes app. Think of a challenge you've faced at work. Answer the following:

What was the **Situation**?

What was your **Task**?

What **Actions** did you take?

What was the **Result**, and how can you make it measurable?

Now try saying it aloud. Does it flow? Practice makes perfect!

Handling Curveballs: Unpredictable Questions

Some interviewers love throwing curveballs to see how you think on your feet.

Q: "If you were a tree, what kind would you be and why?"

Your SMART Approach:

Be **specific**. Choose a tree that represents qualities they'd value in the role.

Keep it **relevant**. Tie it back to the job.

Example Answer:

"I'd be a redwood tree. They're resilient, grow steadily over time, and support entire ecosystems. Similarly, I thrive on long-term growth, adapt well to challenges, and enjoy fostering collaboration within a team."

Pro tip: Smile! Questions like these are often about gauging your composure more than your answer.

The Power of Follow-Up Questions

An often-overlooked skill in interviews is asking **your** questions. SMART candidates don't just answer well; they inquire thoughtfully.

Great Questions to Ask:

"What does success look like in this role over the next six months?" (Measurable and Time-bound!)

"Can you share how the team collaborates on cross-departmental projects?" (Relevant.)

"What's the company's vision for growth over the next five years, and how can this role contribute?" (Specific and Achievable.)

These questions not only showcase your interest but also position you as someone who's already thinking like a part of the team.

Wrap-Up: Leave a Lasting Impression

As the interview concludes, you'll likely hear, "Do you have anything else to add?" This is your final moment to shine. Use it wisely.

SMART Closing Statement:

"Thank you for this opportunity. Based on what we've discussed, I'm excited about how my skills in [specific area] align with your team's goals, especially in [measurable result you'd contribute]. I look forward to the possibility of contributing to [specific achievement or goal they've mentioned]."

End on a note of enthusiasm and alignment.

Final Play: Your SMART Cheat Sheet

Here's a quick recap to keep in your back pocket:

Specific: Tailor every answer to the role and company.

Measurable: Quantify your accomplishments whenever possible.

Achievable: Show you're realistic yet ambitious.

Relevant: Keep your answers aligned with the job description.

Time-bound: Highlight recent wins and future goals.

Practice these principles, and you'll walk into your next interview feeling unstoppable.

Offers, Exercises, and Winning Sample Answers: Your Interview Toolkit

Welcome to the next phase of mastering interviews! In this chapter, we're diving into practical exercises and simulations to equip you with tools that can turn any interview into an opportunity to shine. You won't just *read* about answering questions; you'll actively practice, reflect, and refine your responses. Let's create a space where preparation meets confidence.

Warm-Up: The Mirror Test

Before we get into the nitty-gritty, start with a quick self-assessment exercise. Find a mirror or use your phone's camera. Look at yourself and answer this question:

"Why do you want this job?"

Notice your posture, facial expressions, and tone. Do you look confident? Do your eyes light up with enthusiasm? Or do you seem hesitant?

Here's an example of how you might sound:

Unpolished Answer:

"Well, it seems like a good opportunity, and I like the industry."

Polished Answer:

"I'm excited about this role because it aligns with my expertise in project management and my passion for creating impactful campaigns. At my previous job, I led a team to deliver a marketing strategy that increased engagement by 30%, and I see opportunities to bring similar results to your company."

Feel the difference? Now, it's your turn. Write down your answer and rehearse it until you sound like the polished version.

Exercise 1: The STAR Technique in Action

Behavioral questions are a staple of interviews. The STAR method—**Situation, Task, Action, Result**—is a tried-and-true framework for crafting compelling answers. Let's practice with a classic:

"Tell me about a time you faced a challenge at work and how you handled it."

Scenario: Imagine you were tasked with leading a project where two team members had conflicting ideas. Use the STAR framework to respond.

Situation: What was the context?

Example: "In my previous role as a project manager, I led a team working on a client's product launch. Halfway through the project, two key team members disagreed on the creative direction."

Task: What was your responsibility?

Example: "My role was to mediate the conflict and ensure the project stayed on track while maintaining team morale."

Action: What steps did you take?

Example: "I scheduled a meeting to let each team member present their ideas. Then, we discussed the pros and cons as a team and aligned on a solution that combined elements from both approaches. I also set clear milestones to monitor progress."

Result: What was the outcome?

Example: "The final campaign was completed on time and exceeded the client's expectations, increasing their sales by 20%. Both team members appreciated the process, strengthening collaboration for future projects."

Now it's your turn. Write your response using the STAR method for a challenge you've faced. Once done, rehearse it aloud.

Simulation 1: Rapid-Fire Questions

Let's simulate a quick round of commonly asked questions. Answer each one on the spot, using the tips provided to refine your response.

Q1: "What motivates you?"

Pro Tip: Tie your motivation to the company's mission or role.

Example Answer:

"I'm motivated by solving complex problems that deliver real value. For instance, in my last role, I revamped a supply chain process that reduced delays by 15%, which directly impacted customer satisfaction."

Q2: "Why should we hire you?"

Pro Tip: Emphasize your unique skills and their relevance.

Example Answer:
"You should hire me because I bring a blend of creativity and analytical thinking. For example, I designed a content strategy that not only increased web traffic by 40% but also boosted conversion rates by 25%."

Q3: "How do you handle stress?"

Pro Tip: Share a practical method you use to stay calm and productive.

Example Answer:
"I handle stress by prioritizing tasks and maintaining open communication. During a high-pressure product launch, I created a detailed timeline, delegated responsibilities, and checked in regularly with my team. This approach ensured we met our deadline without compromising quality."

Exercise 2: Personalizing Sample Answers

Take one of the questions from the rapid-fire simulation and rewrite the sample answer to fit your own experiences. Use this format:

Start with a brief introduction.

Provide a specific example.

End with a positive result.

Once written, practice delivering your answer aloud until it feels natural.

Simulation 2: The Unexpected Question

Some interviewers throw curveballs to assess your creativity and composure. Let's simulate a quirky question:

Q: "If you were an animal, what would you be and why?"

Your Goal: Use this question to highlight a quality relevant to the role.

Example Answer for a Leadership Role:
"I'd be a wolf. Wolves are collaborative, strategic, and lead their packs with a balance of strength and empathy. These are qualities I strive to bring to my leadership style."

Now you try! Choose an animal (or a similarly unexpected metaphor) that resonates with your skills and values. Write your response and rehearse it with a friend.

Practical Exercise: "Match the Metrics"

Employers love measurable results. Practice identifying numbers or outcomes that elevate your answers.

Scenario: You're asked, "What's your biggest accomplishment?"

Basic Answer:

"I successfully launched a new product line."

SMART Answer with Metrics:

"I successfully launched a new product line that achieved $500,000 in revenue within its first six months, exceeding our target by 20%."

Take five minutes to brainstorm three accomplishments you're proud of. For each, write down:

What you did.

The measurable impact.

How it aligns with the job you're applying for.

Simulation 3: The Follow-Up Challenge

Interviews often end with, "Do you have any questions for us?" This is your chance to shine as an engaged and thoughtful candidate. Let's simulate a follow-up scenario.

Q: What would you like to ask us about the role or company?

Generic Question: "What's the company culture like?"

Winning Question:

"What aspects of the company culture do you think have contributed most to its growth over the past year, and how does this role play a part in continuing that success?"

Take a few moments to craft three thoughtful follow-up questions you can ask in your next interview. Make sure they reflect genuine interest and align with the company's goals.

Practical Exercise: Practice with a Partner

Grab a friend or colleague and ask them to play the interviewer. Provide them with 5-10 questions from this chapter. Record the mock interview, then review the recording to identify areas for improvement.

Common Mistakes to Avoid

As we wrap up, let's look at pitfalls many candidates face and how to avoid them:

Overloading Answers with Details:
Solution: Stick to the STAR method and keep answers concise.
Failing to Quantify Success:
Solution: Always include measurable results.
Skipping the Research:
Solution: Study the company's values and recent achievements to align your answers.
Forgetting to Prepare Follow-Up Questions:
Solution: Have at least three thoughtful questions ready.

Final Challenge: The Ultimate Simulation

Here's your ultimate test. Simulate an entire interview from start to finish:

Prepare answers to 5 key questions.

Rehearse a professional introduction and closing statement.

Practice answering an unexpected question.

End with three follow-up questions.

Once complete, rate your performance on a scale of 1-10 in these areas:

Confidence

Clarity

Relevance

Measurability

Wherever you scored below an 8, go back and refine your approach.

Closing Thoughts

Preparation is the key to interview success. By practicing exercises and engaging in simulations like these, you're not just preparing to answer questions—you're building the confidence and adaptability that employers value most.

Now go ahead, take these tools, and ace your next interview like the star you are!

Chapter 5: Playing to Win: Mastering Virtual Interviews and AI-Powered Assessments

In the ever-evolving world of recruitment, the year 2025 has ushered in a paradigm shift in the hiring landscape. Companies are increasingly adopting virtual interviews and AI-powered assessments, not merely as a matter of convenience, but as a necessity driven by globalization, hybrid work models, and advancements in technology. For candidates, this shift presents a double-edged sword. On one hand, it opens up opportunities to showcase skills from anywhere in the world. On the other, it demands mastery of new strategies to navigate these technologically charged hiring processes.

This chapter is your playbook to excel in virtual interviews and AI-powered assessments, arming you with actionable insights, strategic tips, and the confidence to not just participate but *dominate*.

The New Face of Interviews

Traditional in-person interviews, with their handshake dynamics and in-the-room energy, are becoming increasingly rare. Virtual interviews conducted on platforms like Zoom, Microsoft Teams, and Google Meet are now the norm. But these digital interfaces come with their own set of challenges:

Body Language Constraints: Subtleties like posture and eye contact are harder to convey.
Technical Glitches: Audio lags or video freezes can disrupt your rhythm.
Perceived Disconnection: Building rapport through a screen often feels less natural.

Meanwhile, AI-powered assessments have risen as a pre-interview gatekeeper, analyzing everything from a candidate's personality traits to problem-solving abilities using advanced algorithms.

Decoding AI-Powered Assessments

AI-driven assessments are no longer just about multiple-choice questions. They leverage machine learning to evaluate:

Behavioral Patterns: Analyzing how you respond to hypothetical scenarios.

Communication Style: Gauging clarity, empathy, and persuasiveness through written or spoken responses.

Cognitive Abilities: Testing logic, creativity, and problem-solving prowess.

These assessments often feel impersonal but are remarkably accurate. They create a data-driven snapshot of your potential, removing biases but also eliminating the chance to rely on charm alone.

Your Play: Prepare with Purpose

To ace AI assessments:

Familiarize yourself with the company's values and tailor your responses to reflect them.

Practice with simulation tools designed for AI-based tests.

Highlight problem-solving and critical thinking, as AI algorithms reward structured and logical answers.

Step 1: Setting Up Your Virtual Command Center

Your surroundings play an underrated but crucial role in virtual interviews. A well-organized environment signals professionalism and preparedness.

Lighting Matters: Position yourself in front of natural light or use a ring light for even illumination. Avoid harsh shadows.

Background Check: Use a neutral background or a virtual one that reflects a professional ambiance. Avoid distractions.

Audio and Visual Quality: Invest in a good-quality microphone and webcam. Test them before the interview to ensure crisp clarity.

Pro Tip: Adjust your camera to eye level. This creates a natural line of sight, mimicking face-to-face interaction and establishing a stronger connection.

Step 2: Mastering the Tech Tango

The biggest faux pas in virtual interviews stem from technical issues. Here's how to stay ahead:

Platform Proficiency: Familiarize yourself with the interview software. Know how to mute/unmute, share your screen, and adjust settings.

Backup Plan: Have a contingency in place—your phone as a hotspot, a secondary device, and a list of the interviewer's contact details.

Dry Run: Conduct a practice interview with a friend or mentor to identify potential hiccups.

Step 3: Communicating Confidence Through a Screen

The lack of physical presence doesn't mean you can't exude confidence.

Micro-Expressions Count: Smile genuinely, nod at appropriate moments, and maintain consistent eye contact by looking into the camera rather than the screen.

Clarity is Key: Speak slightly slower than you might in person to counteract potential audio delays. Enunciate clearly.

Energy Amplification: Virtual settings can dampen enthusiasm. Compensate by modulating your tone and showcasing energy in your voice and gestures.

Step 4: Winning with Storytelling

AI assessments and virtual interviews alike value the STAR (Situation, Task, Action, Result) framework for answers. However, storytelling adds a layer of relatability.

Anchor Your Stories: Begin with a brief context (Situation), clearly outline your responsibility (Task), and dive into actionable steps (Action). Conclude with measurable outcomes (Result).

Make It Visual: Use descriptive language to paint a picture. For example, instead of saying "I improved team performance," say, "By implementing a weekly check-in system, team productivity increased by 20% within three months."

Connect to the Company: Highlight how your story aligns with the company's values and goals.

Step 5: Building Virtual Rapport

Building rapport in a virtual setting is an art form. You can achieve it through:

Mirroring: Subtly mimic the interviewer's tone, pace, and demeanor.

Active Listening: Nod, paraphrase their statements, and ask clarifying questions to show engagement.

Strategic Icebreakers: Start with a light, professional comment about shared interests or the company's recent achievements.

Step 6: Managing AI-Powered Feedback

Some companies provide immediate AI-generated feedback post-assessment. Here's how to make the most of it:

Analyze Patterns: Identify areas where you excelled and aspects that need improvement.

Adapt and Overcome: Use feedback to refine your approach for the next round or future interviews.

Maintain Resilience: Remember that AI feedback isn't personal; it's an opportunity to grow.

Step 7: Turning Challenges into Advantages

Virtual interviews and AI assessments are designed to test adaptability. Use the format to your advantage:

Leverage Notes: In virtual settings, you can discreetly refer to notes. Organize key points in bullet form to maintain a conversational tone.

Showcase Digital Savvy: Seamlessly navigate screen-sharing tools to highlight your portfolio, graphs, or project overviews.

Emphasize Soft Skills: AI assessments often miss nuanced interpersonal skills. Subtly bring these into focus during follow-up interactions.

Step 8: Post-Interview Power Moves

Your performance doesn't end when the screen goes dark. The post-interview phase is critical to cementing a lasting impression.

Follow-Up Email: Send a personalized thank-you email within 24 hours. Reference specific moments from the interview to show genuine engagement.

Feedback Requests: Politely inquire about areas for improvement. This demonstrates humility and a growth mindset.

LinkedIn Connection: If appropriate, connect with the interviewer on LinkedIn, thanking them for their time and reiterating your interest.

The Winning Mindset

In the era of virtual interviews and AI assessments, mindset matters as much as skillset. Adopt these mental habits:

Embrace Curiosity: Treat every interview as a learning opportunity.

Be Authentic: Authenticity resonates even through a screen. Don't over-rehearse; let your true self shine.

Cultivate Confidence: Confidence is magnetic. Believe in your preparation, and it will reflect in your delivery.

Game-Changing Tools for 2025 and Beyond

Maximize your readiness with cutting-edge resources:

AI Practice Platforms: Tools like Pymetrics and HireVue offer simulated AI assessments.

Virtual Mock Interviews: Platforms like Interviewing.io pair you with industry professionals for feedback.

Tech-Enhanced Presentations: Tools like Prezi or Canva elevate your visual storytelling during screen shares.

Virtual interviews and AI-powered assessments are no longer hurdles—they're gateways to opportunity. Mastering them requires not just technical proficiency but also the ability to adapt, engage, and excel in a digital-first world.

By following this playbook, you'll not only survive the hiring process of 2025 but thrive in it. Remember, every interaction is a stage, every question a chance to shine, and every assessment an opportunity to prove that you're not just ready for the future—you're leading it.

Play to win.

Excelling in Online Interviews and Adapting to AI-Based Hiring Tools

The hiring landscape has shifted dramatically in recent years, with online interviews and AI-based hiring tools becoming standard practices in the recruitment process. By 2025, studies predict that over **85% of companies** worldwide will rely on these technologies to enhance efficiency and expand their talent pools. Navigating this landscape requires a blend of technical proficiency, strategic preparation, and adaptability. This guide provides practical strategies, real-world examples, and insightful data to help you stand out and secure your next role.

The Rise of Online Interviews and AI Hiring Tools

Online interviews save time and money for both employers and candidates. In addition, AI tools streamline the selection process, enabling companies to focus on top-tier talent.

Online Interviews: Platforms like Zoom, Microsoft Teams, and Google Meet dominate virtual hiring. A survey by Gartner found that **92% of companies** used video interviews at least once during their hiring processes in 2023.

AI-Powered Hiring Tools: Companies increasingly use tools like HireVue, Pymetrics, and LinkedIn Talent Insights to screen candidates. For example, HireVue's AI algorithms analyze verbal and non-verbal cues during recorded interviews, processing up to **25,000 variables** to generate a suitability score.

This shift demands that candidates excel in both the human and machine aspects of the hiring process.

Mastering Online Interviews: Strategies and Examples

1. Setting the Stage

Creating the right environment for online interviews is crucial. The way you present yourself on camera leaves a lasting impression.

Example:

Jessica, a software developer, secured a remote role at a global tech firm by meticulously preparing her setup. She used a ring light for professional lighting, a neutral background to minimize distractions, and a high-quality microphone for clear audio. Her setup gave her a polished presence, complementing her technical skills.

Tips:

Use a well-lit area with minimal background noise.

Ensure your camera is at eye level to establish virtual eye contact.

Test all equipment (camera, microphone, internet connection) a day before the interview.

2. Adapting Communication Styles

Communication is slightly different in virtual settings due to the absence of physical cues.

Example:

Raj, an MBA graduate, impressed his interviewers by deliberately slowing his speech and pausing between sentences to account for potential audio delays. He maintained eye contact by looking directly at the camera and used hand gestures sparingly to emphasize key points.

Tips:

Speak slightly slower and articulate your words clearly.

Use micro-expressions like nodding and smiling to convey engagement.

Avoid interrupting the interviewer; wait for clear pauses.

3. Leveraging the STAR Method

The STAR (Situation, Task, Action, Result) framework is particularly effective for behavioral questions.

Example:

During an online interview for a project manager role, Ana explained how she led a cross-functional team to meet a tight deadline.

Situation: Her company was launching a new app with only six weeks to prepare.

Task: She was responsible for coordinating teams across three continents.

Action: Ana implemented agile practices and held daily virtual stand-ups to address time-zone challenges.

Result: The app launched on time and was downloaded by **500,000 users** within its first month.

Tips:

Prepare at least three STAR stories that align with the job description.

Incorporate metrics to quantify your impact.

Practice your delivery to ensure your answers are concise and engaging.

4. Managing Technical Glitches

Technical issues are common, but how you handle them can demonstrate your problem-solving skills.

Example:

David, interviewing for a sales executive role, experienced a sudden internet outage. Instead of panicking, he quickly switched to his phone's hotspot and continued the interview with minimal disruption. His calm demeanor impressed the hiring manager.

Tips:

Have a backup device and a hotspot ready.

Inform the interviewer immediately if issues arise.

Apologize briefly and focus on resuming the conversation.

Adapting to AI-Based Hiring Tools

AI tools are designed to assess candidates efficiently and objectively, but they also require a strategic approach.

1. Understanding How AI Assesses Candidates

AI tools analyze verbal content, tone, and even facial expressions. Some systems evaluate cognitive abilities through gamified assessments.

Example:

Mariana applied for a marketing role that required her to complete a HireVue interview. Knowing the system analyzed word choices and tone, she carefully aligned her answers with the company's core values, such as innovation and collaboration. She avoided filler words and spoke confidently, earning a high suitability score.

Tips:

Research the company's values and align your responses accordingly.

Avoid jargon unless industry-specific and ensure clarity.

Maintain a positive tone throughout.

2. Practicing for AI Assessments

Preparation tools can help you simulate the experience of AI-based evaluations.

Example:

Nathan used Pymetrics to practice gamified assessments before applying for an investment banking role. By familiarizing himself with the cognitive games, he improved his reaction times and scored in the top **5% of applicants**.

Tips:

Use platforms like Pymetrics and HireVue practice tests.

Record yourself answering common interview questions to analyze your tone and body language.

Review online forums for insights into specific AI tools used by target companies.

3. Leveraging Data-Driven Feedback

AI tools often provide immediate feedback post-assessment, offering a chance to refine your approach.

Example:

Sofia, a data analyst, received feedback that her answers were too general after an AI screening. For her next interview, she incorporated specific examples and quantified her achievements, such as increasing data processing efficiency by **30%**.

Tips:

Use feedback to identify weaknesses and adjust your preparation.

Focus on specifics: AI systems reward detailed, structured responses.

Seek help from mentors or online communities for actionable advice.

4. Showcasing Soft Skills

While AI excels at assessing technical competencies, it may overlook soft skills like empathy and leadership. Highlight these during follow-up interviews.

Example:

During a final interview for a leadership role, Omar shared a story about mentoring junior colleagues. While this wasn't captured in his initial AI assessment, it resonated with the hiring panel, who valued his emotional intelligence.

Tips:

Highlight examples of teamwork, leadership, and adaptability.

Show self-awareness and emotional intelligence during live interactions.

Don't hesitate to reference real-world situations that reflect your interpersonal skills.

Insights from Data: Why These Strategies Work

Online Interview Success: Candidates who practiced online interviews before their actual sessions were **50% more likely** to receive job offers, according to LinkedIn's 2024 Hiring Trends Report.

AI Tool Optimization: A report by Deloitte found that **80% of candidates** who researched AI tools and tailored their responses improved their hiring chances.

Quantifying Impact: Including measurable results in your answers can increase your evaluation score by **35%**, as per HireVue's internal analytics.

Building Confidence for the Future

Confidence stems from preparation. The more familiar you are with these tools and formats, the more assured you'll feel during the actual process.

Tools to Help You Succeed:

Mock Interview Platforms: Interviewing.io allows you to practice with professionals and receive feedback.

AI Practice Tools: Tools like MyInterview and SHL provide mock assessments.

Online Communities: Forums like Reddit's r/careerguidance or LinkedIn groups offer insights and support from other job seekers.

The Bigger Picture: Beyond 2025

By adapting to these technologies, you're not just preparing for today's job market—you're future-proofing your career. The skills you develop now, such as virtual communication and AI fluency, will remain valuable as technology continues to evolve.

Excelling in online interviews and adapting to AI-powered hiring tools isn't just about ticking boxes—it's about showcasing your adaptability, problem-solving skills, and ability to thrive in a digital-first world. By mastering the nuances of virtual communication, understanding AI-driven processes, and leveraging data to refine your approach, you'll position yourself as a top candidate in any industry.

The future of hiring is already here. Are you ready to rise to the challenge? With the strategies outlined in this guide, your answer should be a resounding *yes*.

Aspect	Key Statistics	Actionable Insights
Adoption of Online Interviews	92% of companies used video interviews at least once in 2023 (Gartner).	Test your tech setup, use professional lighting, and maintain eye-level camera placement.
AI in Hiring	85% of companies expected to rely on AI hiring tools by 2025.	Research tools like HireVue, Pymetrics, and LinkedIn Talent Insights. Tailor responses to company values.
Importance of Preparation	Candidates practicing virtual interviews are 50% more likely to get offers (LinkedIn).	Conduct mock interviews, record practice sessions, and analyze your delivery for clarity and engagement.
AI Feedback Utilization	Candidates optimizing based on AI feedback improve hiring chances by 35% (HireVue).	Use feedback to refine answers; incorporate specific examples and metrics to enhance structured responses.
Soft Skills Impact	Leadership and empathy resonate strongly with hiring panels despite AI focus.	Share stories highlighting teamwork, leadership, and emotional intelligence during follow-up interviews.
Quantifying Achievements	Answers with measurable results improve evaluation scores by 35% (HireVue).	Use the STAR framework with metrics (e.g., "increased productivity by 20%").
Tech Glitch Management	Calm handling of issues improves interviewer perception of adaptability.	Prepare backups (e.g., hotspot, spare device). Stay composed and communicate promptly if issues arise.
Practice for AI Tools	Familiarity with cognitive games improves performance, top 5% outcomes (Pymetrics).	Use simulation tools like Pymetrics and SHL to practice gamified and cognitive assessments.
Future-Proofing Skills	80% of candidates who understand AI tools are better prepared for the hiring process.	Stay updated on tech trends in hiring and continuously adapt your strategies to remain competitive.

Appendices

Appendix 1: The SMART Survival Guide – Quick Prep Exercises for Impactful Interviews

In the relentless rhythm of modern recruitment, efficiency is paramount. As companies gravitate towards condensed hiring cycles, candidates must balance depth of preparation with the practicalities of time constraints. The *SMART Survival Guide* distills preparation into actionable exercises designed to yield high-impact results without exhaustive effort.

Exercise 1: Craft Your Elevator Pitch (15 Minutes)

Goal:

Deliver a succinct, compelling introduction that captures your value.

Instructions:

Who Are You? Start with your professional identity (e.g., "I am a data scientist specializing in predictive analytics…").

What Do You Do? Highlight your expertise and a notable achievement.

Example: "In my current role, I developed a forecasting tool that increased accuracy by 30%."

What Are You Seeking? Conclude with your career aspirations.

Practice Tip:

Record yourself delivering the pitch and refine for clarity, tone, and confidence.

Exercise 2: Master the STAR Method (30 Minutes)

Goal:

Structure responses to behavioral questions effectively.

Instructions:

Pick three challenging scenarios from your work experience.

Break each into STAR components:

Situation: Context of the challenge.

Task: Your responsibility in resolving it.

Action: Specific steps you took.

Result: Quantifiable outcomes.

Rehearse delivering these as concise, narrative-style answers.

Example:

Question: "Tell me about a time you solved a major problem."

Answer: "Our sales dropped 15% in Q2. As team lead, I analyzed data to identify underperforming channels, implemented targeted promotions, and recaptured a 10% market share within six weeks."

Exercise 3: The Industry Insight Drill (15 Minutes)

Goal:

Demonstrate industry knowledge.

Instructions:

Research key trends shaping your industry (e.g., AI adoption in finance or renewable energy regulations).

Prepare two talking points for each:

Trend Insight: "AI has disrupted traditional trading models, enabling predictive analytics."

Your Angle: "In my last role, I piloted an AI-driven tool that optimized our portfolio allocation by 18%."

Practice Tip:

Integrate these insights naturally into responses to display strategic awareness.

Appendix 2: 100 Must-Know Interview Questions – Categories, Examples, and Winning Strategies

Recruiters deploy a blend of standardized and role-specific questions to probe candidates' suitability. This curated list categorizes and unpacks frequently asked questions with strategies to answer them.

Category 1: Behavioral Questions

Objective: Assess past behavior as a predictor of future performance.

Examples:

"Tell me about a time you led a team through a challenging project."

"Describe a situation where you made a mistake and how you addressed it."

Winning Strategy:

Use the STAR method to frame your answers. Ensure the *Result* demonstrates a measurable or qualitative impact.

Category 2: Technical Questions
  Objective: Test role-specific expertise.
  Examples:
  For Software Engineers: "How would you optimize an algorithm for faster processing?"
  For Marketing Professionals: "What metrics would you prioritize for a new product launch?"
  Winning Strategy:
  Be concise and avoid jargon overload. Include examples where you applied the skill in practice.

Category 3: Situational/Scenario-Based Questions
  Objective: Gauge problem-solving and decision-making abilities.
  Examples:
  "If a key stakeholder opposes your proposal, how would you handle it?"
  "Imagine you're tasked with launching a product in a saturated market. What's your first step?"
  Winning Strategy:
  Clarify the scenario to show analytical thinking.
  Outline a clear, logical response framework.

Category 4: Personal Fit and Motivation
  Objective: Determine cultural alignment and enthusiasm.
  Examples:
  "Why do you want to work here?"
  "What motivates you in a professional environment?"
  Winning Strategy:
  Tie your answer to the company's mission and values, while linking them to your long-term goals.

Category 5: Unique Curveball Questions
  Objective: Test creativity and composure under pressure.
  Examples:
  "How would you explain your role to a five-year-old?"

"If you were a superhero, what power would you choose?"

Winning Strategy:

Think aloud to show reasoning and tie your answer to relevant strengths or insights.

Appendix 3: The Success Glossary – Key Terms and Concepts for Future-Ready Interviews

Understanding and using contemporary professional language in interviews signals awareness of evolving workplace norms. This glossary highlights critical terms and how to leverage them effectively.

1. Emotional Intelligence (EQ)

Definition:

The ability to recognize, understand, and manage emotions—both your own and those of others.

How to Use in Interviews:

Frame stories that showcase empathy, adaptability, and interpersonal effectiveness.

Example: "When team tensions rose during a deadline crunch, I facilitated a discussion to address concerns and realign priorities, which improved collaboration."

2. Growth Mindset

Definition:

A belief that abilities and intelligence can be developed through dedication and hard work.

How to Use in Interviews:

Position challenges as learning opportunities.

Example: "I welcomed feedback on my public speaking and joined a workshop to refine my skills, leading to a successful conference presentation."

3. Soft Skills

Definition:

Non-technical abilities like communication, teamwork, and leadership that complement technical expertise.

How to Use in Interviews:

Highlight how these skills amplify technical outputs.

Example: "My technical solution was implemented seamlessly because I ensured cross-departmental alignment through regular check-ins."

4. Data-Driven Decision-Making

Definition:

Making decisions based on data analysis rather than intuition.

How to Use in Interviews:

Emphasize examples where data supported impactful outcomes.

Example: "By analyzing customer feedback data, I identified a common pain point, leading to a 25% reduction in support tickets."

5. Adaptability

Definition:

The capacity to adjust to new conditions or unexpected challenges.

How to Use in Interviews:

Show how you thrived in dynamic environments.

Example: "When my team's resources were cut mid-project, I reprioritized deliverables and achieved 90% of the original goals."

6. Design Thinking

Definition:

A problem-solving approach focused on user-centric innovation.

How to Use in Interviews:

Discuss applying creative, iterative solutions to challenges.

Example: "Using design thinking, I revamped our onboarding process, cutting the learning curve for new hires by two weeks."

7. Agile Methodology

Definition:

A flexible approach to project management emphasizing collaboration, adaptability, and incremental progress.

How to Use in Interviews:

Demonstrate how it improved project outcomes.

Example: "By implementing agile sprints, our team delivered a functional MVP 30% faster than anticipated."

8. Cross-Functional Collaboration

Definition:

Working with diverse teams across departments to achieve shared objectives.

How to Use in Interviews:

Share examples of bridging expertise to deliver results.

Example: "I collaborated with marketing and IT to launch a campaign, increasing conversions by 40%."

9. Diversity, Equity, and Inclusion (DEI)

Definition:

Strategies and practices aimed at fostering an inclusive workplace where diverse perspectives thrive.

How to Use in Interviews:

Articulate how you contributed to or valued inclusive environments.

Example: "I initiated a mentorship program for underrepresented groups, improving retention by 15%."

10. Future-Proofing

Definition:

Preparing for anticipated changes in the workplace or industry.

How to Use in Interviews:

Showcase continuous learning and adaptability.

Example: "To stay ahead in my field, I completed certifications in AI applications and blockchain technologies."

Resources for Success – Apps and Tools to Boost Your Interview Game

Navigating the modern interview process demands more than raw talent. With a plethora of digital tools available, candidates can leverage technology to sharpen preparation, enhance performance, and manage follow-ups effectively. Below is a curated list of apps and platforms tailored to help you excel.

1. Mock Interview Platforms

Interviewing.io

Purpose: Practice live interviews with industry professionals.

Key Features: Real-time feedback, anonymous participation, and recordings for self-review.

Best For: Tech roles, especially software engineering.

Pramp

Purpose: Peer-to-peer mock interview practice.

Key Features: Role-specific sessions (e.g., data science, product management), scheduling flexibility.

Best For: Candidates seeking collaborative practice in a variety of fields.

2. AI-Powered Feedback Tools

HireVue Practice

Purpose: Simulate AI-based interviews.

Key Features: AI-generated feedback on tone, pace, and keyword usage.

Best For: Familiarizing yourself with AI-driven hiring platforms.

MyInterview

Purpose: Practice responding to common interview questions.

Key Features: Video recording, self-assessment, and tips for improvement.

Best For: Polishing video interview skills.

3. Gamified Assessment Prep

Pymetrics

Purpose: Prepare for cognitive and behavioral assessments.

Key Features: Cognitive games that mirror AI evaluations used by employers.

Best For: Candidates applying to industries that value problem-solving and emotional intelligence.

BrainGym

Purpose: Train cognitive agility and focus.

Key Features: Gamified exercises targeting memory, reasoning, and reaction time.

Best For: Candidates aiming to boost performance in cognitive aptitude tests.

4. Resume Optimization Tools

   Jobscan

   Purpose: Tailor your resume for Applicant Tracking Systems (ATS).

   Key Features: Keyword matching, ATS compatibility scores, and detailed optimization tips.

   Best For: Maximizing resume visibility for automated screenings.

   Zety

   Purpose: Create professional, customizable resumes.

   Key Features: Pre-designed templates, cover letter builders, and content suggestions.

   Best For: Candidates needing polished, visually appealing documents.

5. Behavioral Insights and Self-Reflection

   Glassdoor

   Purpose: Research company-specific interview questions and experiences.

   Key Features: User-submitted questions, salary data, and company reviews.

   Best For: Understanding company culture and expectations.

   Reflectly

   Purpose: Journal your thoughts to enhance self-awareness.

   Key Features: AI-driven prompts, mood tracking, and reflective exercises.

   Best For: Strengthening emotional intelligence and stress management.

6. Communication and Presentation Tools

   Grammarly

   Purpose: Ensure polished written communication.

   Key Features: Grammar and style corrections, tone suggestions, and clarity enhancements.

   Best For: Perfecting follow-up emails or written test responses.

   Veed.io

   Purpose: Enhance video submissions.

   Key Features: Video editing, subtitle generation, and formatting tools.

   Best For: Creating polished pre-recorded interview responses.

7. Scheduling and Follow-Up

Calendly

Purpose: Manage interview scheduling seamlessly.

Key Features: Integration with calendars, time zone auto-detection, and customizable meeting options.

Best For: Staying organized and professional.

ThankView

Purpose: Send personalized thank-you messages.

Key Features: Video and text thank-you note creation with tracking.

Best For: Leaving a lasting impression after interviews.

8. Industry-Specific Tools

CodeSignal

Purpose: Practice coding challenges.

Key Features: Custom assessments, peer comparisons, and skill certificates.

Best For: Developers applying to roles with technical tests.

Pitch

Purpose: Create presentations for interviews.

Key Features: Collaborative design, professional templates, and easy integration with data tools.

Best For: Candidates preparing case study or portfolio presentations.

Appendix 4: SMART Success Stories – How Others Nailed Their Interviews and How You Can Too

Success in interviews often hinges on preparation, adaptability, and execution. The following real-world case studies illustrate how candidates used *SMART* strategies to secure their dream roles.

Case Study 1: Sarah – The Finance Professional Who Mastered the STAR Method

Scenario:

Sarah was vying for a senior financial analyst position at a Fortune 500 company. Behavioral interviews were a major component of the hiring process.

Strategy:

Sarah meticulously prepared STAR-based answers for likely scenarios, focusing on measurable results.

Example Question: "Tell me about a time you identified a critical issue and resolved it."

Answer:

Situation: "Our quarterly audits revealed a $1.5M discrepancy in operational costs."

Task: "I was responsible for identifying the root cause and rectifying it."

Action: "I conducted a cross-departmental review, pinpointed duplicate vendor contracts, and renegotiated terms."

Result: "This saved the company $2M annually and streamlined procurement processes."

Outcome:

Her concise, metric-backed answers impressed the panel, leading to a job offer.

Takeaway:

Quantify results whenever possible to enhance the impact of your responses.

Case Study 2: James – The Software Engineer Who Nailed His Technical Challenge

Scenario:

James applied for a backend developer role at a fast-growing startup. The final round involved a technical interview with live coding.

Strategy:

James practiced on platforms like LeetCode and Interviewing.io, simulating high-pressure scenarios. He also reviewed the company's tech stack to align his solutions with their tools.

Execution:

During the interview, he explained his thought process step by step, demonstrating clarity and adaptability.

Instead of merely solving the problem, he proposed optimizations that aligned with the company's scalability goals.

Outcome:

James secured the role and later learned his structured approach set him apart from equally skilled candidates.

Takeaway:

Technical prowess matters, but clarity and problem-solving orientation often tip the scales in your favor.

Case Study 3: Maria – The Marketing Manager Who Leveraged Industry Insights

Scenario:

Maria interviewed for a global marketing manager position. She anticipated questions about navigating post-pandemic consumer trends.

Strategy:

Maria researched industry reports, integrating these insights into her answers.

Example: When asked about her marketing approach, she cited Deloitte's 2023 Consumer Behavior Report, emphasizing the importance of sustainability.

She shared a campaign she led that reduced packaging waste by 25%, aligning with emerging green consumer priorities.

Outcome:

Her strategic awareness and actionable examples led to a successful job offer.

Takeaway:

Demonstrating thought leadership through research-backed insights positions you as a forward-thinking candidate.

Case Study 4: Ahmed – The Consultant Who Turned Failure into Strength

Scenario:

Ahmed applied for a consulting role that emphasized resilience and adaptability. He was asked to discuss a professional failure.

Strategy:

Ahmed chose a story where failure led to growth:

Situation: He launched an initiative to automate reporting, but adoption lagged due to poor stakeholder engagement.

Action: Ahmed conducted a retrospective, gathering feedback to refine the rollout process.

Result: The revised approach increased adoption rates by 70%, earning him a company award.

Outcome:

His ability to reflect, learn, and iterate impressed the firm, securing his position.

Takeaway:

Frame failures as opportunities to showcase self-awareness, problem-solving, and growth.

Case Study 5: Emily – The Graduate Who Won Over AI and Human Interviewers

Scenario:

Emily, a recent graduate, applied for a coveted internship in public relations. The process included an AI-driven assessment and a live panel interview.

Strategy:

For the AI assessment, Emily practiced on platforms like MyInterview, focusing on clear, confident responses.

For the live panel, she prepared stories emphasizing her communication and crisis management skills.

Execution:

She tailored her answers to match the company's values, using words like "collaboration" and "integrity" frequently identified in their job postings.

When asked about a crisis she handled, Emily shared a story about organizing a university event despite unexpected venue issues.

Outcome:

Emily aced both stages, landing the internship.

Takeaway:

Balancing AI optimization with authentic storytelling ensures success across diverse evaluation stages.

These success stories underscore a universal truth: preparation meets opportunity in interviews. By adopting *SMART* strategies and learning from others, you, too, can turn aspirations into achievements.

END